2/18

MG-5.2-0.5 pts

Spotlight on
Kids Can Code

Understanding Coding Through

DEBUGGING

Patricia Harris

PowerKiDS press.

New York

Published in 2017 by The Rosen Publishing Group, Inc.
29 East 21st Street, New York, NY 10010

First Edition

Editor: Greg Roza
Book Design: Michael J. Flynn

Photo Credits: Cover, p. 13 Hero Images/Getty Images; cover, pp. 1, 3–24 (coding background) Lukas Rs/Shutterstock.com; p. 5 Lapina/Shutterstock.com; p. 7 Cynthia Johnson/The LIFE Images Collection/Getty Images; p. 8 vchal/Shutterstock.com; pp. 9, 21 SpeedKingz/Shutterstock.com; p. 11 Sergey Nivens/Shutterstock.com; p. 12 Srijaroen/Shutterstock.com; pp. 14 (sofa), 15 (house) Elvetica/Shutterstock.com; pp. 14–15 (inspector) penang/Shutterstock.com; p. 17 Stock Rocket/Shutterstock.com; p. 19 Valeriy Lebedev/Shutterstock.com.

Cataloging-in-Publication Data

Names: Harris, Patricia.
Title: Understanding coding through debugging / Patricia Harris.
Description: New York : PowerKids Press, 2017. | Series: Spotlight on kids can code | Includes index.
Identifiers: ISBN 9781499427967 (pbk.) | ISBN 9781499428247 (library bound) | ISBN 9781499428827 (6 pack)
Subjects: LCSH: Computer programming–Juvenile literature. | Debugging in computer science.
Classification: LCC QA76.6 H37 2017 | DDC 005.1–dc23

Manufactured in the United States of America

CPSIA Compliance Information: Batch #BW17PK: For Further Information contact Rosen Publishing, New York, New York at 1-800-237-9932

Contents

Eeeek, a Bug!

If you like to talk about using computers, you might have heard the word "bug." A friend might be using an app on a computer or a phone. The friend might say, "This app is buggy!" Your friend isn't talking about a creature with six legs and three body parts crawling on the computer. Your friend isn't nervous about a spy attaching a listening device to the phone. You know your friend is complaining about a problem with the app's coding.

As a debugger, you first need to make sure the problem is with the app and not with the user. It helps if your friend can tell you what happened and what the program did wrong.

"Debug" means to examine the code of a program or app, find out what's wrong with it, and fix it. However, the first step in debugging is to make sure the problem is a bug and not just a user error.

Hopper's Bug

The term "bug" is often credited to Grace Brewster Murray Hopper, an early computer scientist. After teaching at Vassar College, Hopper, a mathematician and physicist, joined the U.S. Navy during World War II. She became a researcher at the Harvard Computation Lab. Hopper helped program the first large computers, and her work led to the creation of a well-known computer language called **COBOL**.

Hopper's bug wasn't really a coding bug at all. Workers in the lab discovered that a dead moth was causing a problem in one of the computers. The workers removed the moth and fixed the problem. Hopper loved telling the story of the moth, but this wasn't actually the first time the word was used. It had previously been used to describe errors found by engineers of all types.

Grace Hopper (1906–1992) helped program early computers for the U.S. Navy, as well as several private companies. She achieved the rank of rear admiral in the navy.

Building and Inspecting

Debugging isn't the same thing as coding. It requires you to think in a different way from the way you would when writing new code. Programming is construction work. You produce a new product and have a lot to show for your work. Being a debugger is more like being a building inspector. Debuggers look closely at the code to find what's keeping the program from running correctly.

Debugging is work that takes a lot of time and has little **output** at the end. Debuggers need to look at the code and make small corrections to the existing program. If all goes as planned, this allows the program to work correctly. Debugging is a lot like testing **software**, but there are differences. Testing finds errors in code. Debugging figures out what the errors are and how to fix them.

Coding a program is a lot like constructing a building. Debugging is a lot like inspecting the newly constructed building for errors or weaknesses.

Debugging Detectives

You can approach debugging by thinking like a computer scientist or like a detective. Computer scientists think, "We haven't used **syntax** correctly in our program." They use debugging tools built into their **programming environment** to find simple code errors, such as a **command** that is spelled wrong. These tools are a little like spelling and grammar checkers in word-processing software.

You can also think like a detective. Detectives are people who ask, "Who did it? How? When? Why?" Of course, a debugging detective does not ask these questions with the intent of a detective trying to solve a crime. While crime detectives are looking for a person or people, debugging detectives are looking for errors in the code.

Breaking the Code

In coding, syntax refers to the commands used in programming languages and how lines are structured. Misspellings and other mistakes in commands mean a program won't work correctly. Some languages use special symbols like { } to surround information that goes together. Other languages rely on spacing.

Coding checkers can help debug a program, but they won't teach you how to become a debugger.

To think like a debugging detective, you must think **systematically**. First, you must know just what the program is doing wrong. You may need to interact with the programmer, people using the program, or documents describing the program. You must have facts. You also have to be able to reproduce the problem and know the steps you took to do so.

Next, write down the problem, list all the facts you have, and form your **hypothesis**. After you write all this down, you really should talk to another person if possible. You can tell them what you know is true, what you think is true, and what you don't know yet. Writing and talking about the problem and the facts help you organize your thinking.

Writing a programming problem down and talking about it with others helps you better understand the problem and how to fix it.

Thinking like a debugging detective means you can't guess about the problem. You need to think of all the different lines of code that could be causing the problem. When you look at a line of code, you ask the question, "Is the problem here?" If the answer is "no," you move on to the next line.

Debuggers keep records of what they have already checked. Even if you have a great memory, taking detailed notes can help you save time and keep your facts straight. If you keep a record of the program you're debugging, you can be sure you're not checking the same part of the code multiple times.

Why is the floor all wet?

The problem in code may not be right at the point where the bug shows up when the program runs. You may also need to look at code that comes before or after that point to fix the problem.

There's the cause!

Breaking the Code

Sometimes you include code others have written in your program. Good debuggers always question code. Question the code you borrow as well as the code you've written yourself.

Debugging Tools

Debugging tools are used by computer programmers when they're testing code. The tools are usually a part of the programming environment. These environments are called **integrated** development environments (IDE). An IDE shows places in the code that have errors in the way words are arranged or spelled. This happens before you run your code.

Here is some code written in Python, which is a programming language that uses common English words for commands. The code was written in the IDE Komodo Edit 9. It has an error.

```
                          getname.py
1   #A program to ask users to enter their name and say hello
2
3   person = input('Enter your name in quotes: ')
4
5   prent 'Hello', person
```

Here is the message Komodo gives you when it looks at your code:

```
13  SyntaxError:Invalid syntax
```

Because the error message says "SyntaxError," you know there's a word or punctuation error, and you know that Python uses English words for most of its commands. You don't know what column 13 has to do with the problem. You can hypothesize that the error might be related to something else in that column, such as the word "prent." You retype the word as "print" and the error goes away!

When there are no bugs, these lines of code allow the computer to greet the person typing **input**. Instead of the syntax error message, the program will respond with a greeting: "Hello, Pat."

Let's Start Debugging

You can download Komodo Edit 9 and add a Python program. You will need to go under the menu choice "View" and choose "View as a language." Then choose Python from the dropdown list.

As you type your program, the text will appear in colors. If you make a syntax mistake, Komodo Edit 9 will give you an error message right away. Different kinds of help or error messages show up when you make a mistake. Now, type in the program below just as it is written. Save the program as nameage.py. Be sure to add the .py **extension** at the end. This tells your computer that the file is a Python file.

```
Text-2.txt*
1   #A program to ask name and age and say hello and then give age
2   person = input('Enter your name in quotes: ')
3   print 'Hello' + person
4   age = input('Please enter your age with no quotes: ')
5   print 'Hi again, ' + person + '! I see you are' ,aje , 'years old.'
6   print 'Next year you will be ',age+2
7
```

What happens when you run this program? It has bugs! Try to follow the suggestions and error messages to debug it.

You need to run your program in the **terminal** mode to see the printout of your program. On Apple computers, open a terminal window and type in the word "Python," a space, and the name of the program including the .py extension. On PCs, open Python in the start menu and type in the file name.

When entered correctly, here is what the on-screen printout from your program should look like.

```
PD-iMac:~ dwightandpat$ python nameage.py
Enter your name in quotes: "Pat"
Hello, Pat
Please enter your age with no quotes: 10
Hi again, Pat! I see you are 10 years old.
Next year you will be 11.
PD-iMac:~ dwightandpat$
```

Based on the code on page 18 your program doesn't look like this! An error message at the end of your program tells you "aje" is not defined. Yes, "aje" should be "age"! But some other small differences exist as well. Run your program again and see if you can fix the other bugs. Good luck.

Finding errors in a program can be as challenging and as fun as developing a new program.

21

Real-World Coding

Software developers test their programs for problems. Once they identify the problem, they debug to find the cause. Sometimes they have to dig to find the real cause. They fix any errors they find, and then they test again to make sure the fixes really solve the problem. They also want to be sure they haven't created new problems with their adjustments.

Testing and debugging can be annoying. Keep calm, don't panic, and keep trying. Sometimes you might even need to ask for help.

Can you debug the rest of the program? Here's some help!

The "Hello" line is missing a ",<space>" and should be:

```
3   print 'Hello', + person
```

The "Next year" line has an extra space before the age and the wrong age. It is also missing the end of the sentence. It should be:

```
6   print 'Next year you will be ', age+1, 'years old.'
```

Glossary

COBOL: Common Business Oriented Language, a type of programming language.

command: An instruction for a computer code.

extension: The last part of a filename that tells what kind of file it is, such as .txt or .docx.

hypothesis: A proposed explanation for why something is happening.

input: Information entered into a computer.

integrated: Different parts brought together to form one group.

output: Something produced by a computer.

programming environment: The set of processes and tools used to create a program.

software: Programs that run on computers and perform certain functions.

syntax: How words are arranged to form a sentence.

systematically: Completing an action in a way that uses a system or a plan.

terminal: A computer screen or window where computer data can be viewed.

Index

Websites

Due to the changing nature of Internet links, PowerKids Press has developed an online list of websites related to the subject of this book. This site is updated regularly. Please use this link to access the list: www.powerkidslinks.com/kcc/debug